Contextual Mission Approach to the Tribals in Assam

Contextual Mission Approach to the Tribals in Assam

An Empirical Study on Mising and Rajbongshi

Enosh Narzary

Christian World Imprints

First Published in 2020 by

Christian World Imprints
Christian Publishing & Books from India
C-3, Wazirpur Industrial Area
Delhi-110052
cwidelhi2017@gmail.com
www.ChristianWorldImprints.com
Phone: +91 11 41526079

ISBN: 978-93-5148-481-3

Printed in India.

DEDICATION

This book is dedicated
to the Missionaries those who have laboured
and died working in Assam, North East India.

CONTENTS

ACKNOWLEDGEMENT

It is indeed proper that the author of this Book would like to express his sincere thanks to those who have helped to complete the final draft of the book. Of which, there are some people without whom this book would not have been possible to bring out in its final shape.

I want to thank Mr Agenesh Basumatary, the teaching staff of Asia institute of Evangelism Bongaigaon Assam, Mr. Paresh Narzary, who graciously gave their valuable suggestions, helped in correcting the work, helped in copying and preparing a final draft by typing this book.

I am indebted to brother Ipen Borgoary, Director of Shalom Communication Ministry Bongaigaon, Assam, India for having played the special role for supervising this book for me. His valuable comments at every stage, going through the pages, giving persistent encouragement, constructive suggestions as and when needed.

I also extend my heartfelt thanks to my dear wife Anju for her patience while working on this book and giving helpful hands in writing some of the materials and encouragement.

And also a special thanks to Mr. And Mrs. T.T. Sor, for the financial help to complete this book.

Last but not the least, thanks and praise be to almighty God for His unseen inspiration as and through my studies and research.

PART - 1

THE TRIBAL IN ASSAM

1. Definition of the term Tribe

Experts define Tribe as a group of people comprising several villages and sharing the same ancestry, language and culture under the leadership of a chief, an indigenous and homogenous group of people who speak a common language having a common ancestors and sharing a particular geographical, social and political background.

2. Major Tribal Groups in Assam

A. RAJBONGSHI

The ethnic origin and development of the Rajbongshi tribe needs more research. The traditional records, social customs, observance of religious rites and rituals, their linguistic peculiarities which can be observed, has undoubtedly been derived from the Koch tribe who are one of the most ancient people of India known with different honorific as well as derogatory names like Kalakeya, Kirata, Kurash, Meche, Ashura, Danava, Rajbongshi, Kshatrya etc. who are predominantly inhabiting in North East India and are scattered elsewhere in entire

Asia. The Aryans influenced over the mightiest fighting against the Koches and encouraged them bluntly to be as the champion and the vanguard of Aryan culture. The reference about the Koches are available in the scriptures and the other works like Kalika Puram, Yoginee Tantra, Rajoupakyan, Darrang, Rajbongshwalis in the writings of native and foreign scholars. Originally the Rajbongshis came down through the foot-hills of Bhutan. As such they were known as the Ut-Koches (Koches from the North) and mingled with the Gotoka families, who were their earlier kith and kins belonging to the same stock (Kiratas) as they were of common origin.[1]

B. BORO

a. The People

The Boros are a group of Tibeto–Burman speaking plains tribal of Assam. They belong to the larger group of Bodos tribe, coming from the Mongolian race. They are known as Kachari in upper Assam. Liguistically, the Bodo includes a large group of people who speak the Tibeto –Murman, language of Nepal, North East Bengal, Burma, Tripura and Assam and includes the tribe like Rabhas Garo, Dimasa, Kachari, Tippera, Lalun Sonowal, Hajong, Mising, Deoris and Chutiyas.[2]

b. Geographical Location

The Boros were once a dominant race in Assam and this is not in any way unlikely by the numerous traces that they have left in the province.[3] The earliest notice of the Boro kingdom was that in Sadiya, who established a powerful kingdom under the name of Chutiyas, but the fact as to how long this kingdom existed can not be traced. The only known fact is that they had a prolonged struggle against the Ahom, a section of and the Great Shan (Thai) race, who drove them out and Boros head to take refuge in Dimapur, the foot hills of Nagaland and eventually the Boro King had to retrieve himself to Maibong and Khaspur (in Chacar) circa 1750 A.D It is noted that in 1790 A.D., the Boro king Krisna Chandra and Govinda Chandra, formally embraced Hinduism and for the process they had to remain inside a large copper image of a cow for certain days. The last Boros King was Tularam Senapati, whose kingdom was merged into the British India after A.D 1854.[4] The foot hills of Bhutan which the Boro people choose for their natural habitation is most suitable for cultivation. Since the Boros depend on cultivation for their livelihood. The nature rivers flowing from the Hills of Bhutan make irrigation easy and this plain was virtually covered with dense forest in the past. At present, three districts of Assam are the sheath of the Boro people , i.e. Darrang, Kamrup and Kokrajhar is the largest Boro concentrated district with its total population of 10,85,976. Out of which the Boro population is 7,66,976. And this district is the main concern of the present study.[5]

c. Sociocultural Life

1. Homestead and Dress: the Boros have their typical homestead with a main dwelling house, the granary, a cow- shed and a parlor which surrounds a courtyard. In addition to that, a garden and a drinking well for the supply of water. The size of the house is built according to the need of the number of people in a family. The courtyard serves as family deity alter, usually built in a corner. During marriages and other special occasions, it is used as the reception place for the visitors and guests. The Boros wear a simple dress. For men, it is a wrapper called Gamsha which covers from loin to the knees, men usually use this Gamsha along with a shirt. Women wear what is known as Dokona, covering from chest to ankle with a blouse and cover with a small scarf on the top. The Gamsha, Dokna and scarf, all are woven by the Boro ladies in their domestic looms with colorfully beautiful designs. Boro women are much fond of ornaments like necklace, earrings, bracelets, bangles of gold and silver.
2. Food and Drinks: Rice is the staple food of the Boro people and they eat three times in a day,. Besides this, they eat vegetables, pulses which are the useful domestic products of their cultivation. They eat almost all kinds of meat of animals, fowl and fish, unless they are considered filthy. Vulture, kite, crow dog, cat and snake are among them. The cow is considered holy and a useful animal, so they do not eat its flesh. Drinking

of the home made rice beer called "Jou" is indispensible to the Boro social life. It is crudely brewed out of rice. After the days hard work, every working person requires a glass or two. The guest and visitors are always welcomed by offering a glass of rice-beer by the family.[6]

3. Social Laws and Customs of Marriage: There is no caste system among the Boros even though their Hindu neighbors do practice caste system. They are ruled by the knightly tribal organization and the existence of this group points toward the existence of the Totamostic Society in the past. Even now, in the interior village one can see the reminiscence of early Totamostic worship. This is a kind of kinship, rather than division the main social groups are : Basumatary, Narzary, Borgoyary, Champramary, Daimary, Goyari,Khaklary, Lahari, Ramchiary, Islary, Iswary, Mushary and Swargwary.[7] Historians believe that the classes mentioned above head their endogamous practice in the early times, though this practice is not prevalent in the modern society. The Boros are a monogamous race; one will hardly come across a man with two wives. Marriage between close relatives is not allowed. Divorce is allowed in certain cases upon the mutual consent but not as a practice. Decision for divorce is considered in the council of the village elder and certain amount of fine is imposed on both the divorcees and usually have to go through certain traditional laws.[8] Both the widow and widower or can remarry but not to the widow of one's younger brother or his wife's own elder sister.[9]
4. Religious Beliefs: In the Boro villages, no idol worship is to be found. But in their mind and imagination, the earth, water, light, fire and sky are a kind of embodied powers and faculties far greater than those of men, along with a vast number of invisible spiritual beings to which they visually called "Mwdai" (spirit) and they are always inclined to think these power and faculties as strong enough to be feared. At a certain stage of time, this idea must have developed and it must have influenced them to have the fear towards nature than to love it. Whenever a person is sick or by Malaria fever, they are front

to attribute this is to the spirits saying that the person is being caught by the evil "spirit" (Mwdai Homdwng). In one way, this could be one accurate expression of the religion of the Boro race and is distinctively what is commonly called 'Animism'. This is further proved by their constant propitiation to keep away these evil-will by frequent offering of goat, pig, poultry, rice, plantain, eggs etc. This practice is still prevalent among the Boro society.[10]

d. Festivals

There is no distinct Boro festival to be described purely for them except that of harvest. During this festival, a lot of rice-beer and pork is consumed, friends and relatives are invited to join in the celebration. Moreover, the celebration of Bihu festival is not exclusively a Boro Festival, this is borrowed from the Hindu neighbors. Because the Bihu festival is observed with great pomp by the Hindus, the harvest festival is now being observed by the Boros during the month of January along with the Bihu festival.[11]

C. RABHAS

a. The background of Rabhas

According to historians, Rabha people came from Tibet. Rabha people derived from Mongolian and on the other hand seem to be derived from Boro. Having come from Tibet, they scattered and settle down in various parts of Assam and Bengal.

b. Geographical Location

All the Rabhas came from the Tibet and they settled in different places. They settled down at first in Assam and later they settled in different places and scattered among them. Some of the districts where Rabha people are living at present are 1. Dhubri 2. Bongaigaon 3. Goalplara 4. Kokrajhar 5. Kamrup 6. Darrang. They never live in the mountains. They like to stay in the valley where there is good water and climate.

c. Sociocultural Life

1. Dress

Rabha people, specially all the woman and young ladies wear and keep alive their cultural dress. Rabha men wear just simple "Gamsa" which is 4 to 5 feet long and 3 feet wide. Rabha women weave this cloth with their own hands. The cloth that the women and young ladies wear is called "Lkun" in Rabha language. They take a kind of long cloth on their neck that is call "Kambang". It has two colours - red and black and that is the main dress for the Rabha women. In ancient times, women and young ladies wore a kind of garland around their waist at least 15 rounds. But in this modern age they prepare a kind of colourful garland, that is made of robe. Rabha people since ancient days has been using the ornaments as gold silver, etc.

2. Food and Drinks

The main occupation of the Rabhas is cultivation. Their principle food is rice. Generally, they eat twice in a day. Lunch and Dinner, according to their tradition they make a kind of alcohol and drink it. But nowadays most of the Rabhas drink tea instead of liquor. These things are being used by the Rabha people. But those who have not accepted Jesus as their personal saviour, they still use the same.

3. Social Laws and Custom of Marriage

As we know that every tribe has their own laws and custom. In the same way, Rabhas have also their own laws. There are different ways to solve problems. Especially for the Rabha Hindu people, we see more traditions and practices. There are some traditions and practices which are done during the marriage function as given below:

a) Both the bridegroom and the bride would take bath early in the morning and make himself/ herself pure on the day of wedding.
b) They make an alter by erecting four banana plants for the wedding ceremony.

c) They place four small water pots on that alter. The water could be taken from any river. When they take water from river/pond, they draw up six times and throw the water downwards. After throwing the water seven times, then they bring the water home.
d) Whether cold or hot that does not matter both bride and bridegroom should take bath before sitting on the alter. It means cleansing up their bodies.
e) The bride ought to come earlier near by alter and stand before the bridegroom comes. The bridegroom and bride will put the garland on each other and sit on the alter and priest does the marriage ceremony according to their customs and traditions. And the priest asks them to put a ring on the other's finger.

4. Family's condition:

Sometimes the Rabha families turn to another family if there is a problem. Especially in the case of marriage, the daughter has to go to the other house as a bride and she will also inherit the property from her parents. Sons will remain at home and they also inherit the property from their parents. The Rabha people give the property to their children irrespective of gender. Be it a son or daughter, they have the right to receive equal property from their parents.

5. Religious Beliefs:

Since old times, the Rabha people have been worshiping idols on a monthly basis. When they see a bog tree they think that there is god and they worship it. They believe in many gods and goodness and worship them. At present, the Rabha people involved in this religious practice are:

a) Christian b) Bwisnob c) Sheeb Sonaton.

6. Festivals:

There is no special festival for the Rabhas. But there are temples in the villages built by them. So, they have festival once in year together. They celebrate festivals called "Chongbai" and worship god. But in the present days. We cannot see more people gathering in the temple. All the Rabha people who are living in Assam, they celebrate all the festivals as other people do and celebrate them as their own. In Assam the main festival is Bihu to which all the Hindus celebrate. This is the short history of the Rabhas.

D. HAJONG

A. Sociocultural Life

1. Dress: The Hajongs have their own hand woven cultural dress and is called "Ronga Patin." It is specially meant for women. For men, there is a smaller and shorter dress which is known as "Hajong Gamsa" that is their cultural dress.
2. Food and Drinks: Rice is there staple food but often they take Roti or bread. They eat almost all the green vegetables and all sorts of meat. They make a kind of liquor and use it. They use it more when there is some festival or celebration.
3. Marriage Customs: According to their marriage customs, before marriage the bridegroom's parents go to bride's home to see and to urge. If it is okay then they will go again for ring ceremony where rings are exchanged between bridegroom and bride. If both families agree, the marriage can be solemnized as soon as possible or according to their capabilities.
4. Religion and beliefs: Most of the Hajong people are Hindus. They worship Shree Krishna. They believe Shree Krishna would provide all the needs of their family and protect them. He gives peace and prosperity. There are only a handful Christians among them.

E. MISING

Mising People and their History

It is often said that Takam people are "the largest Mising people" in northeast India. They have been neglected and marginalized from the mainstream Assamese culture. Lately, several Mising people have formed themselves into groups to assert their native rights and identity. Few have become Christians in the process of cultural assimilation. They have no economic base due to illiteracy, ill- health and dependence on others. Many of them still live in the remote jungles and riverside and survive on bare daily wages. Some who moved to the urban areas have done better. Like all other tribals, their history goes back to China and Mongolia from where they came and settled in the plains of Assam. They have their own tribal deities but are heavily interpolated with Hindu worship practices. Drinking rice beer is customary among all the Mising.

Basic facts and Figures

Mising population is estimated to be 1200,000 people in entire northeast India Out of which, about 115,000 are living in Assam. The rest are scattered in Arunachal Pradesh and Meghalaya. Distribution of Mising people in Assam is

a) Sonitpur 150,000 b) North Lakhimpur 200,000 c) Dhemaji 350,000 d) Majuli area 100,000 e) Jorhat 70,000 f) Dibrugarh 30,000 g) Sibsagar 10,00,000.

The figures noted are from Dr. Bilash Pegu's report on Takam Mising people. In Arunachal Pradesh, they are mostly found in Pasighat, Subansiri and Siang districts.

The Challenge and Task

As most Mising people live in the north bank of Assam, the North East Vision ministry has initiated the Evangelical works among them since November 1, 2005, mainly in north Lakhimpur district of Assam. The Mising people Church has been started in three difference places. The Mising Baptist Church Council is also doing evangelical work in Assam among the Mising people.

F. LALUNG

a. The People The Lalung have migrated from Tibet-Burma group. Originally, they inhabited in the plains and in the range of Brahmaputra valley of Assam. So, they are known as the "plains tribe" of Assam.
b. Geographical Location They are one of the Bodo Kachari language groups whose origins can be traced to the 17th century, when they migrated to the plains of Assam and neighboring

Meghalaya from the Tibetans Mongloid. They are divided into exogamous clans namely, Monrong, Madum, Moloi, Dafan, Halkai, Amehi, Kush, Chalong, Kakhor, Amchong, Darphong and Loron. They also employ titles like Deka, Raja, Bordoloi, Deuri, Senapoti, Konwar, Doloi, Bharali and few others surnames.

c. Sociocultural Life

1. Social custom and marriage: Social custom about marriage, monogamous system are similar to other tribal groups of north east India. Interestingly, those living in the plains are matrilineal while those residing in the hills follow matriarchal system.
2. Food and Drinks: Their principle food is rice. Same as Bodo Kachari, they eat three times a day, and they use a kind of homemade liquor from rice. And use it especially on occasions like marriage, festivals etc. But those who are Christians do not drink it.
3. Religion and Beliefs: Almost all the Lalung people are Hindus. They are very strong in their faith. They trust in Shiva as their God. In other words, they call Shiva as "Kuworchi" and "Tamlong Kubir". They believe that Shiva, their God helps them during troubles, suffering, struggles etc. They worship idols and sacrifice goat and dove etc. Their belief is that through sacrifice sins are forgiven. Lalung people they do not have their own festival. But they observe Bihu as other Hindu people. They observe it in a very special way and take it to be their own festival. They wash up the cowshed and give new robe for every cow and bullock; in the same evening they observe a special Puja which they called it "Tamlong Kubir" Puja. They observe it in the solitary place, especially in the jungle.

G. DEORI

a. Short history of Deoris

The name Deori is traditionally associated with the royal temple of the Chutias of Assam.[12] derived from Sanskrit "Deva Grihika" meaning the Temple Guard.[13] They like to be called themselves as "Gemasayas" meaning the children of the sun and the moon.

b. Geographical Location

They are recognized as one of the plains tribe of Assam. They are mostly scattered in the districts of North Lakimpur, Dhemaji, Dibrugarh, Tinsukia, Sibsagar and Darang. Total population is estimated to be around 50,000. Historians like Brown opined that Deoris migrated from Lohit district of Arunachal Pradesh into Assam. The four sub-clans of Deoris are Dibongiya, Tengapaniya, Borgony. Intermarriage among the sub-sections are prevalent. As regards to their origin, one theory states that they were originally Aryans, moving from central Asia, Mongolia and finally entered into India under the leadership of Debal and Basistha. The descendants of Debal became Deoris the theory said. Aryan connection is made through their folktales which could have come also through their association with the Aryans.

c. Sociocultural Life

1. Dress: In Assam, the Deoris have adopted Assamese dress, custom and to a great extent religion also. Recently, the Deoris are trying to revive the old customs and traditions by which they want to identify themselves as Deoris distinctly.
2. Food and drinks: Their food habits and language confirms their affinity to the tribals of northeast India. Their staple food is rice which they take three times in a day. They take almost all kinds of vegetables as well as almost all kinds of meat. They drink a kind of homemade liquor but the Christians do not use it.
3. Religion and beliefs: Due to their close association with the Chutiyas, who are recognized as "Other Backward Classes" of Assam, the Deoris are noted for their religiosity. They are culturally and religiously allied to the Chutiyas who have embraced Hinduism. They have their distinct culture, language and animistic religion (Kundu Mania) which however has been overwhelmingly influenced by Assamese religion and culture. "Dukia Kinuma" is the creator God Almighty creating the first pair of man and woman. Burma-Burhi is worshipped by

Dibongiyas. However, the four Deori clans have different deities like Bolia, Baba, Mata, Bueha-burhi, Kechaikati or Tamreswari, Sal or Cheng-Konwar.

H. KARBI

a. The people and their background: The Karbis are one of the tribal group in Assam. They originally migrated from Tibeto-Burman group and became the original hills tribe who inhabited in the range of Mikir Hills. The Karbi are divided into three categories - Ronghang, Chingthong, and Amri.
b. Geographical Location: The Karbis are located in the hilly areas mainly in Mikir Hills, nowadays known as Karbi Anglong. The word Anglong means hills. At present three districts of Assam are main sheaths of the Karbi people - Karbi Anglong, north Cachar Hills and Kamrup. Among three districts, Karbi Anglong is the largest Karbi concentrated district with the largest population.
c. Sociocultural life: The Karbis have their typical homestead with a main dwelling house, with a granary, a cowshed and a parlor which surrounds a courtyard. The size of house is built according to the need and the number of members in a family. During winters, a small fire place is erected to warm up at a spot where family discourses held where a lot of advice is given to the youngsters.
d. Dress: The Karbi wear a simple dress. For men, it is a wrap called Gamsha, which covers from loin to the knees. Men usually wear this Gamsha along with a shirt. Women wear a Paning Pekkok covering from chest to ankle with a blouse. The Gamsha and Pekkok are woven by the Karbi ladies in their domestic looms with blue color and beautiful designs. Karbi women are very much fond of ornaments like necklace, earrings bracelets, and bangles of gold and silver.
e. Food and Drinks: Rice is the staple food for the Karbi people and they eat three times a day, besides this they eat vegetables and pulses which are the produce of their cultivation. Drinking the home made rice beer which called Hork is indispensable in the Karbi social life. Apart from the daily use, during festivals

and other happy occasions, it is consumed in large quantities. They also smoke and chew tobacco.

f. Social Laws and customs of marriage: There is no caste system among the Karbis, even though their animistic neighbors have much practices of this system. The main social groups are Kathar, Ingti, Bey, Teron, Timung, Ronghang, Phangcho, Ingjal, Kroh, Phak-Kor, Marme, Keleng and Terang.

g. Family: In the Karbi families, both husband and wife enjoy equal status and make joint decisions but in the cases of conflicting decisions, the husband overrules. Both couples owe responsibility for the family properties. Sons are looked as the sole inheritance of the family property. In the family, in case there are only daughters in the family, parents decide who will be the inheritor of the property. In such cases, the family chooses their son in law to remain with them to look after the old parents and usually the youngest daughter is chosen for this purpose.

h. Religious beliefs: In Karbi villages, no idol worship is found. But in their mind and imagination, the big trees, big rock, air, water, fire and sky are an embodiment of power and faculties far greater than those of humans. With a vast number of invisible spiritual beings, which they visually called Dhindhinic (spirit), they are always inclined to think these powers and faculties as something to be feared. The religion of the Karbi tribe is distinctively what is commonly called "Animism". This is further proved by their frequent offering of goat, pig, rice, eggs, etc. This practice is still prevalent in the Karbi society.

i. Festivals: There is no distinct Karbi festival to be described purely for them except that of the harvest festival of Domahi. During this festival, a lot of rice beer and pork is consumed, friends and relatives are invited to join in the celebration. Moreover, the celebration of Domahi festival is not exclusively a Karbi festival; this is borrowed from the Hindu neighbors, because the Domahi festival is observed with great pomp by the Hindus. This harvest festival is being observed now by the Karbis during the month of January along with Bihu festival

3. Constitutional Status of the Tribals in Assam

The Tribals of India were the original inhabitants of India who are from the Proto-Australians, the Mongoloids, the Nagritos and Dravidians as observed by Ponraj who quotes L. P. Vidyarti, a noted Anthropologist, "The first three (the Austro- Asiatic, the Mongloids, the Dravidians) racial and cultural elements made a great contribution to the formation of the Indian people."[14] As the year passed by, the Aryans conquered them and the original people were made slaves and some are scattered all over India who are now considered as Tribals in their own land. The Indian constitution speaks about the safeguard of very people of India as it is spelt out in the Fundamental rights of the Indian constitution by which it guarantees to promote harmony and brotherhood among all the sections of the people transcending religious, linguistic and regional or sectional diversities. The constitution also recognizes three social categories such as; [15]

1. The Scheduled Tribes (ST)
2. The Scheduled Castes (SC)
3. Socially and Educationally Backward Classes (BC) and Other Backward Classes (OBC).

1. Scheduled Tribe (ST) - Most of the Tribal communities are poor and underdeveloped. They are socially oppressed and economically exploited by the non-tribal people. To ensure protection and help by the Government, they are given an administrative and political concept of listing them as Schedule Tribe, extending them special support for their upliftment and welfare. These groups of people represent 10% of the total population of India.
2. Schedule Caste (SC) - Schedule Caste people are considered as "according to the caste system in India, they are known as "Dalit" or "untouchables". To protect them from oppression, the government extends various privileges for the welfare and development of this section of people.[16]
3. Socially and Educationally Backward Classes (BC) & Other Backward Classes (OBC) - According to the findings of the

government, there seems to be still some communities who are classified as "Backward Classes and "Other Backward Classes" besides Scheduled Tribes and Scheduled Castes". The Mandal Commission recommended to the Government of India several benefits and privileges for the welfare and development of this community.[17]

4. Strength of Christianity among the Tribals of Assam

Over the years, tribals have been subjected to endless harassment, hardships and oppressions by the landlords, merchants, moneylenders, contactors if higher class and to some extent government officials. Thousands of them have been made bonded laborers and slaves and that must be the reason the tribals are uneasy with the Sanskritization of the Hindu Brahmincal religious orders. They are either more favorable to remain as Animist/Tribal religion or prompt to accepting Christian faith. This is obvious from the history of Indian church. Different people's movements came to Christ among various tribal groups in northeast India. Even today Tribals are the most responsive people to the Gospel as compared to other groups of people in India. There are many reasons behind why the Tribals are more inclined to the Gospel

1. It may be to get away from the social oppression, 2. To get deliverance from fear of evil, 3. To live a good moral and dignified life, 4. To get satisfactory answers to their problems, 5. Tribal religions are closer to Christianity than any other Faith, 6. They are simple minded and uncorrupted by other cultures, 7. Their belief in Supreme Being makes them believe in the God of the Bible, 8. Tribals experience miracles through prayers 9. Tribals are psychologically ready for a change.[18]

ENDNOTES

1. Ambika Charan Chaudhury; "Varieties; A collection of ten Articles, "Bholanath Press, Bongaigaon, 1993, pp. 33-44.
2. Kameswar Brahma; "A study of socio-religious beliefs; Practical and ceremonies of the Bodos, Punthi Pustak, Calcutta, 1992, p.1.
3. Sidney Endle; "The Kacharis (Bodo), Low price publications. Delhi, 1990, p. 4.
4. lbid. pp. 6-7.

5. Kameswar Brahma, Opcit., p. 267.
6. Sidney Endle, Opcit., pp. 18-19.
7. lbid. pp. 24-27.
8. lbid. pp. 29-31.
9. Kamewar Brahma, Opcit., p. 75.
10. Sidney Endle, Opcit., pp. 49-50.
11. lbid.
12. Ambika Charan Choudhury, Opcit, pp. 312-35.
13. P. C. Muanthanga, "The harvest filed of Assam." Carey research and communication centre, Shillong, 1996. pp.31-32.
14. S. D. Ponraj, "Tribal Challenges and the church's response." Mission Research and Education service, madras, 1996. p. 25.
15. Ibid. p. 26.
16. Ibid.
17. lbid. pp. 159-169.
18. Ambikha Charan Chaudhury, Opcit., pp. 312-317.

Part – II

RAJBONGSHIS AND THEIR IDENTITY

1. WHO ARE THE RAJBONGSHIS

2. A brief historical survey

The Koch people, who are also popularly known as the Rajbongshis, seem to be the direct descendants of many Rajas and their blood relationship with the royal families. They accepted the rites and rituals that are strictly followed by the Hindu Kshatriyas, especially in the early 20th century under the leadership of Rai Bahadur Panchanan Barman. He is regarded as the father of Rajbangshis in North East India. Hence, they have reasons to socially identify themselves as Kshatriyas and 27th Magh month of Assamese calendar is recognized as Kshatriyas Divos (Festival). At present, they have formed an association which is known as 'Koch Rajbangshis Sonmillon' which was founded by Raja Ajit Narayan Deb; even in West Bengal same association is known as 'Rajbongshi Kshatriyas Samity'. Naturally these people are mostly puritan, dogmatic and emotional but very loyal and mainly rely on their muscular strength and fate. At present, agriculture is their main source of livelihood. They are generally still unfit to adjust to the changing trend of modernization and in the present day intellectual maneuvering and adultery of thought, they are fish out of water. They have, thereby, become easy victims of all sorts of exploitations. They were once rulers and builders but now have become beggars at others door for their very existence. So they are behind in all respects, for this very reasons these people are placed as 'Schedule Caste' in West Bengal by the Government and as the 'Other Backward Class' in Assam, but this recognition by the governments has helped them very little, because the backwardness has taken place by the very hands of bureaucratic government. Though planning and policies are good, they could not touch the very periphery of the problems of their backwardness. In general, these people are systematically derived before government and semi government fields. And that is why 95% of their community are now below the poverty line and there is growing discontentment and agitation which is heading its way. But the intellectuals are utilizing their condition to their benefits, as can be seen in the fabricated news being published in English daily Telegraph dated 12th April, 1983, and in the weekly English magazine Sun Day page 29 of 1st May, 1983.

1. These suggest, without any doubt, that the Kochs were of Mongoloid race very closely allied to the Mechs and Garos and could be found in Jalpaiguri, Kochbehar and Goalpara. The people known as Rajbongshis are either pure Kochs who are of Mongloid elements and usually preponderate.[19]
2. In early times the Kochs and Meches freely intermarried, but the Kochs' conversions into Hinduism has now caused the practice to be discontinued (Gaits History of Assam).
3. In "The Chronicles of the Tepara King", it is said that the word still survives as the designation of a tract in the sub- Himalayan between the Dud Kochi and Arun reigns and the Khamba Limba and Yokha Tribes who inhabited it.[20]
4. Kochs and Kacharis are the same ethnic group and the Kochs are represented by the Kocharis who inhabit in Nowgong, Goalpara, Kochbehar and the neighboring area of Grierson.

5. The transformation of Koch into Rajbongshis, the name by which they are now known in Rangpur, Jalpaiguri and Kochbehar is a singular illustration of the influence exercised by fiction in the making of caste. Now the great majority of the Koch inhabited of Northern Bengal invariably describe themselves as Rajbongshis or Banga Khariya (Domestic Census Report of India, 1891).
6. The Kochs are one of the most ancient of the people of India, their linguistic affinity is with mech Kocharis." (Delton).
7. The Koch is a tribe and their language is allied to the Kocharis, Tripurius, Garos etc. It belongs to the Bodo language group. (Dr Iscot Marbaniang: Assam in a nutshell).
8. "The Koch empire under King Narnarayana and his brother Sulashwaja during second half of the 16th century is another great achievement of the Indo-Mongoloid Bodo people and preparations for this climacteric rise were going on for some centuries before that age,. If the assumption is warranted that the Licchavis, Koliyan and Vaijis of north Bihar in the 6th century B.C. were of Indo-Mongloid origin, pure or meted then it is quite to think of north Bengal as much as Assam having an Indo-Mongloid population from quite early times.[21] These are the glaring examples of calculated foul play by the so called intellectuals over the ignorance of the backward but straight forward people like Koch Rajbongshis. They were once protectors of art, literature and religion of all and built kingdoms but now in flotation like gypsies, nomadic tribes for shelter here and there; because they are pushed out from this ancestral holdings by East Bengal / East Pakistan / Bangladeshis. Due to this type of political crime imposed upon these people.[22] who ruled systematically king in Eastern India specially undivided and greater Assam. During the reign of Maharaj Narayanan, who was senior to his contemporary Akbar of Delhi, was later known as Vikramaditya of Kamrupa. Chilarai - the younger brother of Maharaj Narayanan is now regarded by historians as one of the greatest general that the world has ever produced in ranking only with Shivaji and Napoleon. He was a writer and scholar and was a disciple of Shri Sankardev. Though Mararaj Narayanan was a legal emperor of Kamata Empire, Chilarai

was a chosen the de facto king but was very loyal to his elder brother Narayanan. During the golden regime, the Ahom, Kachari, Jainatia, Manipur, Sylhet, Gonda etc. kingdoms were subjects to the vast Kamata Empire. Chilarai constructed the present Kamakhya temple in 1565 AD. The great Vaishnava saint, Shri Sankardev, Shri Madavdhev and Shri Damodhardev propagated Neo-vaishnavism during that time. Many literary works in Assamese language of the Koch kings. As a matter of fact, the present Assamese state is the outcome of the Koch kings because prior to Maharaj Narayanan in 16th century there was no Assam and Assamese people but various separate kingdoms existed. As a matter of fact, the whole of the ancient literature of Assam is full of appreciated references to the benevolent Koch rulers of the past. This should awaken an interest in the minds of our educated upcoming generation in the historical literature of our country and should serve as a help in Kamrup / Komota witnessed anarchy at the end of 15th century AD due to ruthless attack of Nawab Hussiain Shah of Gonda and set up some colony of Afghans. Among these chiefs and their followers by far and numerous and powerful were the Kochs who gradually united under the authority of Biswa Singha. The founder of Koch kingdom of modern period Biswa Singha was succeeded by his grandson Nara Narayanan as king and his third son Sukladhwaj also known as Yonaraj. Sukladhewaj was a great warrior and assumed the title Sangram Singha. He became the commander in chief of Koch army which according to Akbarnama, consisted of 4000 horses, 200,000 infantry, 700 elephants and 1000 war boats. With this capacity, Sukladhwaj deployed such skill and promptness of action that he was nick named Chilarai or the kite king. Chilarai led his impregnable army into the Ahom kingdom and conquered it after a long and fierce resistance. This triumph of Chilarai over the powerful Ahom kingdom was significant in his military career. Next he sent his expeditions to Chachar, Kairam, Dimapur, Manipur, Tripura/Jayantia and Sylhet etc. Independent kingdoms were subjugated and annexed under the Koch Kamata Empire. Chilrai also invaded Nawab of Bengal from the east while Raja Mansingh who was in command of imperial army advanced from the west by which the Nawab of Bengal was easily defeated and the kingdom was divided between the Koch king, Nara Narayanan and Akbar, the emperor of Delhi. As a military prodigy, Chilarai had demonstrated his superior strategic genius and the unfailing striking power of the Koch army. The west country bounded in the west Mithila, in east extreme frontier of Assam, in the north the Himalayan range, and in the south by the shores of the Bay of Bengal. Chilrai consolidated the power of the newly established Koch kingdom eliminating all the disrupting elements within what was in his infant kingdom. His brother Nara Narayanan had a dream to establish a Hindu sovereignty over entire eastern India including north Bengal and north Bihar which was the ideology possessed by deep learning unusual personality and of the firm lover of his brother. Chilrai won for him the most coveted position of Dewan of the Koch Empire at its zenith.

a. **Social and Cultural life:** It is believed that the Indian culture is derived from people group such as Dravidians, Aryans, Mongoloids, Australoids. The culture is based on the very life of the ritualistic worship of Shiv and Parvati. The culture of Kamota kingdom spread from Koch Bihar (north Bengal) Medinapur to Calcutta. The famous song of Rajbangshis is a "Lokh Geet" which is famous for the people of Assam. The Rajbongshis are still using the Lokh geet-the folk songs, lokh Nritya-the folk dances, Tantra Mantra-the magic practices. In early times, the Kochs and Meches freely intermarried but this connection has been diverted due to the Kochs conversion into Hinduism. Meches and Rabhas are said to be admitted into the category of Rajbongshis on the ground of conversion into the Hinduism. But the process of being Hindu is to get themselves to Modahi and Saraniya. According to the Karnal Delton, the Kochs are originally from Dravidian area.

b. **Dresses of Rajbongshis:** The unique dress of Rajbongshis woman is called "Patar." They weave this for themselves with flowers on it. Gamocha (a kind of towel) is worn by men and it is also woven by the women folk. Every woman has to wear their Patami before their marriage. For a young girl who does not know how to weave Patani, it will be hard to find a suitable partner and are not given the title "Tatati."

c. **Food habit:** Sidal, Matikalai (pulses) with mutton, bamboo shoot, dry fish, Tapola rice, dried vegetables.

d. **Titles used by Rajbongshis:** Adhikari, Koch, Konwar, Karzee, Kathaniar, Karghoria, Giri, Sarkar, Chaliha, Choudhury, Thakuria, Trata, Tohbildar, Tarafdar, Roy, Barman, Ting, Rajbongshis etc.

e. **Religion and worship:** In many areas, the Koch Rajbongshis worship Shiv- Parvati as home God and Goddess. At the time of marriage, the elderly women sing traditional songs and welcome Shiv and Parvati to the household. They also worship spirits and deities. The Kochs do not worship the Sijou (Cactus plant) like the Boros, but they use the Tulsi plant during their worship. The Kochs highly respect their mothers, so worship the Goddess Mansa and identify her as their mother. Along with this, many families worship the destroyer goddess "Bisho Hari" as a "Kuldev". They also worship domestic Gods and Gods outside their home. For the domestic God, Pujas are performed at home and for the Gods outside home, they performed Pujas at the designated places in the village by offering chicken, goats, pigeons etc. Before harvesting the paddy, they offer a Puja of thanks giving to God for the protection of their field from rain, storm, wild animals and other natural calamities. After performing the Puja in the field, they bring a portion of paddy from the field covering with banana leaf and performs another ritual at home and keep it. They also observe the Bhohagi Bihu, where they prepare eight items and cook as a celebration of harvest. The mixture is called At Korai Bhat. They also prepare Sona Bhat which is a preparation of sticky rice, boiled in water covered with banana leaves.

f. **Language and Literature:** According to the linguist Greason, the history of Assamese language is older than the Bangla language of Bengal language. Rajbongshi language is also one of the ancient languages of India which ultimately transformed into Kamrupee language. According to the 1891 census, Rajbongshis speaking population was, **Goalpara - 2,92,800, Jalpaiguri - 5,68,976, Cooch Behar - 5,62,500, Darjeeling - 47,835, Rongpur (East Pakistan) - 20,37,460**. The total population comes to 35, 90,341. The linguistic survey of India by Greason also shows the same figure. There are lots of Sanskrit words used in Rajbongshis language. However, there seems to be no doubt that the true Kochs were of Mongoloid race very closely allied to the Meches and Garos, who are found in Jalpaiguri, Cooch Behar and Goalpara. Rajbongshis are either pure Kochs whose skin is dark or a mixed race of Mongoloid elements as their physiognomy shows.[23] The Kochs and Kacharies are the same ethnic group and the true Koches are represented by the Kacharies who live in Nowgong, Goalpara, Koch Behar and the neighboring countries. The language of the Koches, the dominating and ruling tribe in the great Koch kingdom, was derived from the ancient prestige and power, long enough to be visited by an English man Ralfitch in Queen Elizabeth's time. It would seem then that the language spoken in the ancient Koch kingdom which extended from the Himalayan to the Bay of Bengal was the Koch and Brahmaputra and Surma valley ought to show how far the Koch element still persists, how far it has been obligated by inter marriage with the Indian immigrants.[24] The Assamese people are highly indebted to the Koch king for their language, literature, culture and arts. The Koch is a martial race and makes fine soldiers. They had ability to form army for Maharaja Narayanan and conquer many kingdoms. For defense of the country and for the protection for wealth and home, they fought bravely and valiantly against the Moguls, Ahoms and the

Bhutias for about a century. Due to warrior nature, they were called Jharus (Jhar-Forest).

g. **Economy:** It is a known fact that almost all the tribals rely on their muscular strength and fate. They seem to work hard but do not know to invest their time and talent in proportion to work. To this, Rajbongshis are of no exception; they are generally apathetic to intellectualism and education. There is no doubt on their hard work but economically they are marginalized. This is partly because of their illiteracy and ignorance on the facilities being offered by the government and party due the exploitation of the government officials where the intellectuals and rich masses join their hands. Rajbongshis rely on cultivation and rice is their staple food. Handful of them do some petty business but there is no way for them to complete with other businessmen like Rajasthanis or Marwaris. Their mental makeup is still unfit to adjust to the changing trend of modernization. And thereby have become the easy victim of all sorts of exploitation and conspiracies. They were once rulers and builders but now they have become beggars at others door for their very existence. In general these people are systematically deprived. That is why 95% people of this community are now lying below the poverty line.[25]

II. Constitutional Status of Rajbongshis: As per the Indian constitution which was constituted and came in action under the chairmanship and guidance of former President of India Dr. Rajendra Prasad in 1950, Indian Tribal people have been divided mainly in four categories (1) Scheduled Tribe (ST) (2) Scheduled Caste (SC) (3) Other Backward Classes (OBC). Accordingly, by way of reservations in the central government, they are given a status to enjoy some welfare and benefits granted by the government. The total population of Koch Rajbongshis in present Assam constitutes about 33%. In India constitution, the Rajbongshis came under the category of Other Backward Classes (OBC) till 1990. Rajbongshis seem too silent regarding their status in India constitution. But with the formation of "All Assam Koch–Rajbongshis Kshatriya Sanmiloni" in the recent years, the Rajbongshis have accumulated their strength for gathering more facilities from the central government of India and claimed to consider them as Schedule Tribe (ST) as there are more constitutional safeguards in this category. This movement flourished only for very short duration as their demand to be included in ST status was very strongly objected to by other tribes who have the same status. Their claim could not last long against the strong opposition of various tribes such as Bodo, Garo, Karbi, Mising, Rabha, etc. To be considered and to be included in the Scheduled Tribe status. The Rajbongshis still pursue with a stronger movement for their claim and have another demand for greater status as statehood known as Kamotapur.[26]

III. The Strength of Christianity among the Rajbongshi

The unreached population by the Gospel in five districts of lower Assam is 26,15,676 out of which Christian percentage would be 0.1% in Dhubri district – 9,39,360; Kokrajhar district 1,70,178; Bongaigaon district 3,73,486; Goalpara district 3,28,708; Barpeta district 8,03,944. In the lower Assam, especially in Bongaigaon district, some people have responded to the Gospel but present upsurge of banning conversion to the religion i.e. to Christianity is strictly enforced by making rule of their own. The rule to accept Christian faith is that either risk paying a fine fixed by village committee or be expelled/excommunicated from the village. However, there is still a favorable response towards the Gospel if the message is being carried and one among them are Rajbongshis.[27] Moreover, till today nobody is doing an extensive research on the Rajbongshi tribe and the literature being very limited, it is very difficult to calculate the strength of Christian population among Rajbongshis. But it can be envisaged that only a handful of missionaries are working among Rajbongshis in Assam.

ENDNOTES

19. Ambikha Charon Chaudhury, opcit. 318- 320.
20. Opcit., pp. 321-328
21. Lbid., pp. 20-22

22. Lbid., pp. 312
23. Lbid., pp. 321- 328
24. Lbid., pp. 339- 345
25. Lbid., "Varieties." pp. 21-22
26. Lbid., pp. 20-23
27. M. Vijayanunni, "a state District profile : census of India 1991" Indian Administrative Service register General & Census commissioner, India, N.D. pp. 104-105.
28. Opcit. pp. 20-23
29. Vijayanunni, Opcit. pp. 104- 105.

Part - III

MISING TRIBE AND THEIR IDENTITY

1. A brief historical survey: The Mising people are the largest plain tribal people concentrated in upper Assam. From the time of their ancestors, they have been residing near the Brahmaputra river of Assam. The Mising people are inhibiting on both sides of the Brahmaputra river in the middle and upper Assam and Arunachal Pradesh (the Arunachal Pradesh Mising people are called Ab Mising). The population and the cultural life of the Mising people bears distinguished characteristics. They were located from the south bank of Brahmaputra from Golagha district onwards and north bank of Brahmaputra from Sonitpur district to Sadia (Tinsukia District). The distance is about 300kms. The distribution of the Mising here is scattered in the districts of Sonipur, Lakhimpur, Dhemaji, Tinsukia, Dibrugarh, Sivsahar, Jorhat, Golaghat and Majuli river Island in the state of Assam and Pachighat, Subonsiri, Siang districts in the state of Arunachal Pradesh. Occupation of the Mising people is mainly agriculture and allied enterprises viz. pisciculture, piggery, poultry, sericulture and handloom etc. Mising were popularly known as 'Miris' in the plain tribe of Assam. It is said that the

Mising migrated from the hills of Arunachal Pradesh into the plains of Assam about eight centuries ago and continued to do so, till the first part of the 21st century. The Mising have their own literature committee called Mising Agom Kebang. The Mising language was introduced in 130 primary schools in Mising areas since 1986. The Mising people mostly have been inhabiting on the bank of the river Brahmaputra. Needless to say, they have been the worst victims of recurring floods and erosion - a problem that has been aggravated by the ineffective and unscientific flood control measures adopted by the Assam government. Although the Mising people are living in the Brahmaputra valley since the ancient times, they have not been given permanent settlement rights. Because of the lack of permanent settlement rights, the Mising have not been able to obtain loans and other benefits from banks as well as government sources due to which it has not been possible for them to take up commercial or industrials enterprises for their economic upliftment.

Culture system of Mising tribe: Dance and music are integral parts of the life of the Mising people. They have retained their age-old traditioaal dance. The dances are accompanied by songs and music. The songs include Oi Ni: Tom A: Bang, Kaban etc. Songs are sung on all social occasions. The musical instruments include Dumdum, Marbang, Lc, Nong, Dendum, Dentug, Dumpang, Tapung, Tu, Toog, Gungang, Pempa, Pi, Li, Rai, Rcg, Yoksa etc.

Dress of Mising people: The Mising people have their own colorful traditional dresses. They weave out the cloths in their traditional looms; Gadu, Mibugalung (Missinggaun) Ege, Dumrc, Ugon, Po Tum, Scng, Matagapa, Tapum, Gon-Yab, Potoi, Ri, Bigascng, Yamno, Sogon, Paycg Gasor, Niscg, Kimbu Gasor, Scgung, Potali, Gapa, Gero, Kegrecg, Kebbung etc.

Ornaments of Mising people: During year, the Mising people observe various festivals according to their traditional beliefs. Their festivals are Porag, Amrag, Dobur, Ali-Ayelvgang, Uroposum etc. Amrang: In this festival, food is prepared with the harvested crops and it offered to ancestors. Po: Rag: It is one of the biggest socio-religious festivals of the Mising people. A Murong house is necessary for performing this festival. The host village invites the youth (Mvmbvr Ya : Me) organization from a neighboring village to participate in every aspect of the festival. A priest known a Mibu is invited who conducts the prayer to Sedi-Mclo, D:Nyipo:Lo etc. About 10 to 20 pigs are sacrificed in the name of different deities in the festival. The Mibu, at night, signs A:Bang leading the dancing youth forming in a circle. The festival runs for three consecutive days. The whole village, irrespective of age, sex and caste enjoy the feast and dance. Dobur: It is one of the most important and rigid festivals of the Mising people. It may be organized by a single family or collectively by several families. It has different types of performances for different purposes. Burto Dobur is performed only on the occasion of bloodshed of some grade.

1. Arug Dobur is called the agricultural Dobur is performed by individual families to ward off attack of pest and pestilence from the fields.
2. Ko: Son Dobur is performed by the hunters to save them from the evil spirits during hunting in the jungles. Chickens are usually sacrificed while performing this festival.
3. Ali-Aye Lygang is a showing festival of Mising people. Ali-Aye Lygang stands for first roots and fruits and Lygang for sowing. The oncoming of the 'Ahu' and 'Bau' season is marked with the celebration of Ali-Ayelygang. The Mising people believe Wednesday to be the day of Hindu Goddess Laksmi. On that day, the head of the family marks the sowing of the seeds in their fields, with a handful of seeds, a Yokpa, Apon, Purang, Take, Peero, Sipag, Onno carrying in a Ygyn. Using the Yokpa, he clears a small patch of land in the eastern most part of the field and it is then decorated with the Peero and cotton threads in a square or a circular patter (size about 2 feet to 3 feet). The Apong, Purang, Take and Sepak are placed at appropriates places, within the decorated area. Then the seeds are sown over the area and chants are offered to the forefathers Sedi-Mc:Lo, Karsing-Kartak, Do:Nyi Po:Lo etc. To bear witness to the sowing seeds, into the womb of mother earth for abundant crops, good harvest etc. in

> the day time, the woman get busy preparing Appong and Purag. In the evening hours, the head of the family again prays to their forefathers including Koje-Yaggo. After the feasting, merrymaking starts in the form of Gumrag-So:Man. Urom po: sum. In this particular festival, the departed forefathers are satisfied by scarifying pigs after the harvest to prevent those incurring diseases, accidents or some uncommon occurrences.

Language and Literature: The language of Mising people belongs to the Tibeto- Burma branch of Sino-Tibetan or Tibeto-Chinese language family. The Mising language had originally no script of its own, but Roman scripting in modified form is being now used for their language in primary schools in the Mising dominated areas in Assam with effect from October, 1986.

The Mising literature was composed mainly of oral literature such as folk songs, folk tales, etc. The written literature emerged first in the wake of the movement led by the Mising Agom Kcbang – the Mising literature organization. At present, the Mising literature has been growing rapidly and the Mising Kcbang is making uniting effort in inspiring writers, compiling and publishing literary works in different fields of literature. With the spread of education and increase in the number of Mising readers, the Mising language is expected to attain maturity in the near future. The Mising Agom Kcbang and all the Mising people have considerable responsibility to enrich and develop their language.

Mising House: The Mising people build their dwelling house on raised platforms about 5-6 feet above the ground. A typical house is sometimes as much as 30/40 meters in length and the breadth is about 20 feet. The roof is thatched and the walls and doors are made of bamboo. A Mising house should have five layers above and five layers below. There is usually no inner portion but there are several fireplaces - Mcram, separated by small partitions. There are two main doors one in front and other at the back of the house with one of two outlets in the sides. All other essential household equipments and articles are kept inside the house making special provisions.

Food and drinks of Mising People

1. Rice is the staple food of the Mising people. Agricultural lands are mainly suitable for cultivation of Ahu paddy, hence the people depend mainly on Ahu rice. They now also do wet cultivation. Along with rice, they take locally produced vegetables, creepers and eatable roots. Fowl and pork are their delicious diet. Fish are taken when they are available.
2. Apong is considered to be the most important and prestigious item for entertaining guests and relatives. Apong-Nogin and Po:Ro are prepared for fairs, festivals and for guests.

Disposal of the dead: Burial is the prevailing practice among the Mising Community. Every village has a common burial ground called Ago-Gound and nature of death after keeping the corpse in a long coffin called Rungkug and purification ceremonies are performed afterwards such as Tiloni Mahekia and Dongang.

Economic System: The Mising people are agriculturists and agriculture is their main source of livelihood. When they lived in the hills, they adopted the shifting cultivation. After their migration to plains, they adopted settled cultivation. They produce rice, mustard oil seeds, black pulse, potatoes and vegetables. Rice is produced mainly for domestic consumption, whereas mustard seeds, black pulse, potatoes etc. are used also for commercial purpose. Most of their methods of cultivation are however still crude and primitive, hence the yield is quite low. The produce is not sufficient to meet their requirements round the year. Further, a considerable quantity of rice is used by every family for the purpose of brewing rice beer. The Mising woman have a vital role in improving the economic condition of the family. They participate in every aspect of agricultural work. Moreover, the young woman practice Rykscng and they earn much from it. They all rear pigs, buffaloes, goats, cows, fowls. These animals are needed not only for cultivation, but also for selling in the market for quick cash. Pigs are needed mainly for sacrificing to the deities. The Mising people are almost always exposed to floods and erosions that damage their land, crops. These factors cripple their economy day after day. Hence, the Mising economy is still very poor.

Religion and Worship: The Mising are animistic in their religious outlook. Their religious philosophy is mainly based on animism. They believe Sadi Mc: Lo to be the earliest worldly beings representing male and female. They consider Do:Nyi and Lo:Lo as their Mother and Father respectively. They also believe in the existence of Abo Tani, Karsing, Kartag, etc as their forefathers from immemorial past. Apart from the above deities, the other deities like Yari, Muglvng, Csar, Asi, etc are considered to be the spiritual beings possessing power much greater than man.

The Mising people are superstitious. The minute affairs of individuals and even for the greater and more important events of the world, they are considered to be under the influence of divine spirits and agents. They call the spirit as ui. There are different types of ui such as Talccng, Dobur, Urom, Po: Sum, Gumvn etc. Sacrifice of animals is performed to pacify them. The Nibu is known as the head priest of the society. He is believed to be empowered with some supernatural powers and on all important religious occasions he conducts as chief priest.

Now, Hinduism has been the main influence in the religious beliefs of people. The worship in the Namghar, recitation of Kirtan or Bhagwat etc are some of the examples. However, it has not touched the core of the society particularly those living in the remote corners and witchcraft is not uncommon.

(A) Total population of Mising People

(1) Census report: According to TMPK, MMK estimate the total population of the Mising people in Assam is more than two million in 1989 as per their memorandum submitted to the Honorable Chairman, three members expert committee on Bodos and other tribal issues demanding creation of an autonomous state for the Mising people of Assam. (Memorandum pg 4)

Brief information about Mising population in AssamNorth East India.

(1) Sonitpur district 100,500, (2) Lakimpur district 200,000. (3) Dhemaji district 200,700. (4) Majuli River Island 80,000. (5) Tinsukia district 100,000. (6) Dibrugarh district 50,000. (7) Sivsagar district 100,000. (8) Jorhat district 100,5000. (9) Golaghat district

100,000. (10) Pachighat Subansiri Siang in Arunachal Pradesh 10,000. This is the total population of Mising people in northeast India.

Transportation and Communication in a Mising Village

Most of the Mising villages are located on the both sides of the Brahmaputra river. Being badly flood- affected some Mising people were allotted their land to established villages near the border area at the Nagaland and Arunachal Pradesh by the government of Assam. Most of these habitations are located in remote, interior and inaccessible areas, far from district headquarters. After the independence of India, till now proper medical facility is not available at Mising dominated areas. Basic health and medical services are very poor in Mising villages. No proper road, transportation or communication facilities like phone, internet are available in Mising village areas. As a result, many of the Mising people feel neglected by the government of Assam since ages past.

Strength of Christianity among Mising People

Apart from Arunachal Pradesh, there are total eight districts of upper Assam where Mising people are living. Total population of Mising tribe is 1,200,000. There are total 6,000 villages, in which, only 37 small churches are planted. There are total 5, 963 villages that have no church and also there is no Mising church in the three districts. The Mising people are very receptive and responsive to the Gospel of Jesus Christ at the moment.

The North East Vision Organization of Bongaigaion is concentrating on the district of north Lakhimpur and also in other regions of Assam. There are many privileges in working among Mising tribe in Assam.

Part - IV

EVALUATION OF THE OLD AND NEW MISSIONARY APPROACHES

1. WHAT IS MISSION AND EVANGELISM

A. Mission: The word 'Mission' describes the very nature of God who creates and reveals. And the Church in its very nature is Missionary 'which exists by its mission' and so the mission creates the Church and the Church creates the mission. It will be convenient to put the scholars view on the mission as:

a. "Mission arises from God's nature reproduced and reflected to the whole Church through its conformity to Christ and in its participation in the Holy Spirit's seeking reform of human society and exercising the gift of spirit. So, creation may reconcile to God.[28]

b. "The Mission of the Church is Evangelism alone. This is a wrecked vessel. God has given me a lifeboat and said to me, Moody, serve all you can'.[29]

c. "Mission in Christ's way is God centered, joyfully entering, through thought and action, into God's ceaseless, sacrificial, loving activity to reconcile all that He created to Herself.[30]

Finally, one can not define Mission accurately since no definition and it will be better on the part of the believers to use the Biblical image, symbols events of narrating the Cross, the Resurrection, the Ascension, Pentecost and the second coming of Christ Himself.

B. EVANGELISM: The word itself is from the Greek noun 'evangelize' which is generally translated as 'Gospel'. Denoting the good news of God's coming in the 'flesh' in Jesus Christ and worked out in his death and resurrection, extending to the outpouring of the Holy Spirit and the coming into being of the Church. The verb means to proclaim good news where the emphasis was on speaking, announcing or proclaiming a message. The English word 'evangelize' is translated of the New Testament Greek words 'Evangelizes thai' (verb) and 'evangel ion' (noun) the noun means 'good news' and is translated in most of the Indian languages e.g. Happy news (Hindi and Bengali). The Old Testament "Septuagint' suggested this in Psalm 40:10, the psalmist says, 'I have spoken of evangelized of thy faithfulness and thy salvation" and in Psalm 96:2, he says the Lord, by telling or evangelizing about His salvation day to day. The New Testament uses the word "evangel ion" 72 times and frequently with the verbs "preach" proclaim, indicating that evangelism in the New Testament was normally done by preaching Jesus in the early period. The New Testament speaks of Jesus going into Galilee evangelizing and saying the Kingdom of God is at hand. (Mk. 1:1). The disciples going to the villages evangelizing and healing everywhere.

(Luke. 9;6) The early Christians evangelizing the world.(Acts 8: 4) Phillip in Samaria "evangelizing or proclaiming concerning the Kingdom of God and the name of Jesus Christ" (Acts 8;12) the Apostles "evangelizing many village of Samaritans" (Act 8: 25) and Philip proclaiming the Good News to all the Towns along the Palestinians coast (Acts 16:10). What were all these evangelists doing? Preaching the good news tidings, announcing the Kingship of Jesus and calling people to repent and believe. We are certainly not to suppose that everybody who was evangelized was also converted to Christianity. Evangelizing does not mean converting; it means proclaiming or telling the message so that people understand it and can make their response. For some, it will be rejected thus evangelism in the New Testament essentially means proclaiming, speaking, heralding or announcing the good and important news of Jesus Christ.[31]

II. Theological foundation of Christians Mission

If you ask most of the Christians to say what they understand by the word 'Mission' their answer would be in terms of text entrusted to the Church. The Roman Catholic have used the term "Missio'dei" (the Mission of God) and describe the Father, the Son and the Holy Spirit related to one another. It is relational movement. The idea of relationship must be in the front of our mind, if we are to understand about God, His Kingdom and His Mission. The Father sends the Son and the Holy Spirit, this is what the God who is one in three is like in Himself. This movement of sending out is revealed both in the creation of the world and coming out of the Son to live a human life on earth. The 'Mission' therefore, describes what God is like and also what the Church is like, in which Missionary exists by Mission, as fire by burning. Moreover, mission creates the Church, so it comes before the Church doctrine and Theology. Theology exists to serve the Church in the Mission of God. Mission bridges the gap between the Church and the Kingdom of God. The Goal of the Church is not of its own good but the rule of God; the Church was founded for a future in the Kingdom of God and so it is for all humankind, to which the Christians have produced a very different outlook of Mission.

III. The Old Missionary Approaches

A. Acculturation or Westernization: The development of Indian way of understanding the Gospel is perhaps more important. Theologies grow out of people's experience of Jesus Christ in their own society. V. Chakkarai has said, "Life must form its own body and water of life must cut its own channel". When Indians first began to write Theology, they thought in terms of translating Western Theology or restarting the western theology so that other Indians could understand it more easily. They began to turn to the Hindu religious tradition for inspiration. Some like Dayannand Sarasvati turned to the Vedas and thought that for Hindus, they should be replaced with the Old Testament. We have noticed that some people thought it to be a dangerous idea which would lead to syncretism. Bishop A.J. Appaswamy turned to the Hindu Bhakti tradition as the basiS for his theology. Bhakti means a loving devotion to a particular deity. The Bhagwat Gita (as the Lord's Song), the most famous of the Hindu scripture expresses Bhakti to Lord Krishna. Bishop Appaswamy saw Christianity as Bhakti to the Lord Jesus Christ. One of the most important 20th century Indian Theologians was P. Chenchaiah of Madras who reinterpreted the teachings of St. Paul on the 'new creation' in a way that was meaningful. The Indian Christian Institute of Religion and Society in Madras have been developing an Indian Theology of Social Witness.[32]

18th and 19th centuries witnessed a great spiritual movement in European history known as Pietism Movement. This movement strongly emphasized the personal religious right based on the experience of the individuals. The most significant and prominent exponent of this movement was Philipp Jacob Spanner (1635-1705), a Lutheran Pastor. As a result of this movement, the European Church began to realize its obligation for Evangelization for which it had enough self confidence. The idea of Christians was that they have everything to offer to the rest of the world. Education for the ignorant, wealth for the poor, ethics for the amoral, peace for the warlike, civilizing and the skill for the savages, religious for the godless and also English to replace the barbaric languages.[33] For a certain period, this method of evangelism proved successful because of political, economic and religious power they enjoy in many nations of the world due to colonialism. However, people slowly began to question this method, as it looked up on other culture as godly and superior and therefore, their culture must be accepted by all nations as soon as they embraced Christian faith. [34]

B. Education and Literature

Education and literature were the main factors that have brought about a change and helped people to introspect on the difference in communities. It is no wonder that when the Missionaries had their own objectives in educating the people, namely to enhance their work in evangelism by enabling them to read and write but at the same time also enabling the Christians analyze their own socio culture life. The relationship between Education and evangelism was implicit in the understanding of the missionary Gospel. But in many areas of Mission field in India, the early missionaries failed to train new Christians in the areas of Mission and Evangelism, where many western missionaries could not be successful in their mission work,[35] These missionaries who introduced the western education through English medium schools, particularly they rendered unique service towards the promotion of vernacular schools and for the upliftment of the tribal areas of Assam. In 1844, the American Missionaries under the Rev. Cutter established 14 Schools in Sibsagar. During 1853-1863, Walses Missionaries started many schools in the Khasi-Jaintia hills, Garo hills, Darrang and Nowgaon districts of Assam. The first Assamese newspaper 'Arunodaya' was first published by a Missionary Society. They entered into the interiors of the hills and plains and learned many languages. They also wrote books in many languages; the following books may be mentioned.

1. Grammatical notes in Assamese Language by Rev. Nathan Brown (1848), 2. Grammatical notes by Rev. H. Halvorsrud (1938), 3. A Brief Vocabulary in English and Assamese by Mrs. Suson Andward (1864), 4. First Assamese Dictionary by Dr. Miles Bronson (1867). Due to the sincere efforts of the Missionaries, many tribal literatures reached the average man. It did not only help the advancement of the literature but also ushered in the growth of a standard language that was understood by everyone. The Serampore trio - Carey, March Man and Ward in collaboration with an Assamese Scholar Atmaram Sharma translated the whole Bible into Assamese and published in 1813. Though the spread of elementary education was the main objective of the Missionaries enterprise yet they established some high schools with the arrow's object of giving a high standard of education to tribal children. The main contribution of the early missionaries in the field of education are: 1. Starting Charity Schools, 2. Provisions for fixed hour of schooling, 3. Establishing printing press, 4. Establishment of teacher's training schools, 5. Provision

for financial grant to schools, 6. Constructions of school buildings, 7. Taking responsibility of educating the orphans, 8. Compulsory Biblical teaching.[36]

IV. THE NEW MISSIONARY APPROACHES

A. Co-existence

Assam is a multicultural state like other states of India. It socially is a fusion of many races and religions. So Assam can be well termed as mini India. Only an estimated 4% of its 26 million people are Christians. In such a context, mission work has to be done in a way that does not break the peaceful social fabric. Roger Bowen has said, "If we look at any culture in the light of the Gospel, we see that has some features which are praiseworthy, some features which are intolerable and some which are tolerable".[37] For instance, if we look at tribal culture in the northeast India, we find that they have very strong family relationship with the elderly. They also respect the sacredness of nature. So the Churches and missionary organizations should appreciate these values of other cultures and societies when presenting the Gospel, such that social harmony can be maintained. The New Testament itself is multicultural and does not approve of only one culture (Acts 10&15 Chapters). This teaching of New Testament drives the churches to reconsider the old Missionary approaches of attacking the other culture in presenting the Gospel in non-Christians world. Some of the cultural values that may be objectionable in evangelization should be reformed and reconstructed in the light of the Gospel.

B. Cross-Fertilization: In 1913, Bishop Lukas incorporated the Christian sacraments into the rights of Tanzanian traditional religion, not in order to abolish African society but to baptize it for Christ. Paul wrote in Romans 9-11 Chapters that different cultures can learn and support mutually and precisely because they are different. So, each culture can give something to the other like plants can be cross-fertilized with the other. Each culture can praise God for its differences and thereby enrich our forms of worship. So, cross fertilization and not de-construction, should be the aim of Christian Missions in India, particularly in the western part of Assam.

C. Inter-Faith Dialogue: In view of interfaith dialogue, the following definitions should give an inclusive idea. Israel Salvanayagam defines dialogue as "an intimacy of personal relationship, enjoyment of each other and sharing of knowledge, experiences, problems, and resources."[38] According to Paul E. Knitter, dialogue is "The exchange of experience and understanding between two or more partners with the intention that all partners grow in experience and understanding."[39] And according to S.J. Samartha, "Inter-religious dialogue is a mood, spirit, an attitude of love and respect towards neighbors of other faith."[40] There is no one particular universally targeted goal of dialogue. There may be one or many goals of dialogue depending on the situations, perspectives and issues where a dialogue is concerned. However, since dialogue is a human effort and there can be no dialogue without human participation, the ultimate aim would be, directly or indirectly, to uphold humanity as a whole. Even though inter-religious dialogues may take place in the form of discussions, around theological concepts or mysterious aspects of religion, its ultimate goal is to serve human concerns such as justice and peace, freedom and security, dignity and respect. In other words, to put in a nutshell, the ultimate aim of inter–religious dialogue is to establish the Kingdom of God here on earth.

A critical dialogue does not involve an exchange of ideas while avoiding critical questions. He says that dialogue concerns truth and includes analysis, answers, objections, judgement. So, a critical dialogue consists of four things:

(a) An examination of that which others actually believe
(b) Articulation of one's own belief
(c) Readiness to learn from another, which concerns those aspect of the critic that are true and continue to obtain
(d) Open discussion on mutual criticism with concerns and practices of belief[41]

ENDNOTES

30. Roger Bowen, "so I send". ISPCK, Delhi, 1998, p. 11
31. Ibid., p. 14.
32. Ibid. p.

33. Richard W. Bowie, "light for the nation," Haggai centre, Singapore, 1992, pp. 1-3.
34. L.Piruet, "Christianity Worldwide. " ISPCK, London. 1989, p. 70.
35. Roger, Op cit. p. 8.
36. Op cit.
37. Paresh C. Narzary, an Assesment of the Impact of Christianity on the Boro people of the Kokrajhar District".
    An unpublished Thesis Submitted to Union Biblical Seminary pune, 1995. p. 32.
38. Lakshahira Das, " Elements of Education – 1," Saraighat Phototypes printers, Guwahati, N.D. pp. 115-117.
39. Roger, Opcit. p.82.
40. Siricharan Iswary, "A study of the Concept of the "the Incomparable God" in deuteron Isaiah and iin the Boro traditional religion and its implication for intern- religious dialogue" An unpublished M. Th. Thesis submitted to senate Serampore Collage, 2000, p. 75.
41. Ibid. p. 76.
42. Ibid. p. 77.
43. Ibid.

Part – V

THE CONTEXTUAL MISSION APPROACH

A. Indigenous Evangelism

Down the history of the Church, it has been seen that churches and missionary organizations have made several attempts to evangelize the world. People were very optimistic that the world will soon be Christianized but it did not happen. The World Missionary Conference took place in Edinburgh in 1910 and its slogan was "the Evangelization of the world in this generation. Even the word Missionary has became unpopular as am equivalent to 'Colonialism'. This is reflected in the titles of some books that appeared in 1960s, e.g. 'Mission in a time of testing', 'Mission at the crossroads', 'The unpopular Missionary', 'The ugly Missionary', 'Missionary go home' etc. One thing seems to have been left out, and it is the idea of indigenous evangelism. Indigenous evangelism could be described as an approach of evangelization in which the Missionaries are from the new converts themselves. The advantage here is that the missionaries here know the culture of the target group and they, in return, feel at home with Missionaries. In 1912, a person called Ronald Allen complained that Mission Churches in most parts of the world were; (a) not indigenous or not rooted in the local culture (b) dependent on parent churches for the money, ideas and leaders (c) all alike so failing to God given riches.[42] It was noticed that most of the churches in the mission field have been built in European style, worshiped God, liturgies and tunes, followed rituals and behavior and were dependent on foreign leadership. Thereby churches appeared more western than indigenous. According to Allen, "a truly indigenous church is a group of believers who live out their life in the pattern of the most local society."[43] Some of the most important characteristic of indigenous evangelism are as:

1. The Church here begins independently without the work of missionaries 2. The Church is not founded, but it is planted in the soil of the local culture 3. New converts are taught simply or clearly so that they can easily translate the Gospel into living and doing 4. The church should use its own financial resources and discover its own spiritual gifts to strength its life.[44]

Therefore, our churches as far as possible should be culturally rooted.

B. Acculturation: God's personal self disclosers in the Bible were given in the terms of the hearer's own cultures. If this was not so, we could not have understood God with our limited minds. When God wanted to enter into correct relationship with the people of Israel, he used the "ancient Hittite Suzerain treaty" with His vassal. Similarly, the New Testament languages and thought forms are rooted in both Jewish and Hellenistic's cultures. Peter and Paul's journey to the Jews and to the Gentiles, when carefully analyzed and constructed, highlight their sensitivity to the audience and their willingness to work within the cultural context of the target audience.[45]

In future, work needs to be added in relation to Mission within culture what we term as intercultural mission. If is Jesus sending us into the world just as he came, our role needs to be taken seriously and there is need for the Church to manifest its existence in more concrete cultural and national identities. We need to understand our own culture, in an effort to communicate with Jesus Christ from within our own setting. This is far more natural process of communication which could be referred to our "intracultural" mission. This does not stand in opposition in any way to "crosscultural" mission but only seeks to off-set an unnecessary imbalance.[46] Culture is very much a part of God's concern for His people. He Himself introduced that the fall of humans also results in the fall of cultures.

But that is, in no way a sanction for the detachment of Christians from local culture. Jesus Christ fully identified Jewish culture. Not because it was a perfect culture but because it was his own culture. The fact is that he sent us into the world which implies, he has called us to be part of our individual cultures and thereby eventually contribute to the redemption of culture, to conform with the ultimate Kingdom cultures. The attempt to use the local culture as a vehicle to communicate the Gospel to non-Christians has attracted opposite reactions from the Christian community. If culture is not defined, one can not see how many persons could avoid contact with it, if he or she is seriously concerned with communicating an important message that must be understood by the receiver. In this process, we are involved directly and indirectly with human cultures, but many still attempt to stay above the culture line and deal only with matters of the Soul. But that effort is hopeless, as is the effort of a social scientist who eliminates God from this world and tries to explain Christianity in cultural terms only. The ministry of the Gospel cannot communicate without concerning himself with the cultures, because communication and culture are inseparable. Just as Jesus became flesh and dwelled among human beings, a proportion about truth must have culture. Incarnation to meaningful, hence by adopting the cultural patterns and world view of the target audience, the communicator can effectively communicate the Gospel. What is actually involved here is not the altering of the essential content of the Biblical thought behind the message, but the enclosing of the message in culturally relevant thought verbal form. We have no right to change the content of the Gospel, which could be a betrayal of our trust, but we have the obligation to fit the same content in a culturally meaningful form such that the message would be clearly understood by the hearers.[47]

In chapter two of this research, it is discussed that the Rajbongshis and the Mising have very rich culture of their own.

Therefore, acculturation is presenting the Gospel within their own culture, e.g. the way of worship known as 'Kirtan' or 'Nam' (a way of worshiping god among Rajbongshis) can be adopted while presenting the Gospel.

C. Education and Literacy: The early Christian missionaries came to India to teach and preach the Gospel in obedience to the great commission of Jesus Christ. "Go, therefore, and preach all nations, baptizing them in the name of the Father and of the Son and of the holy Ghost" Mk. 28:11, the appealing condition of compartmentalization of the society prevailing due to casteism, superstition and suppressions of human rights have made us reach the poor and the downtrodden of the society through education where missionaries are working to uplift and ensure social justice. The spade work done by the early Christian missionaries strand as monuments even today in different places of the country. The notable contribution made by these missionaries, e.g. Serampore trio, Alexander Duff and Bishop Coldwell to the cause of education, is due to their vision to reach the people through education. Despite government's opposition, they fought their way to achieve their goal of delivering people from spiritual, mental and social bondage. In the year 1813, the British parliament introduced a change in the East India Act, which enabled the missionaries to impart the westernized education to the Indian citizens. Those missions responsible during the 19th century, were London Mission Society, S.P.G. Lutheran Churches, the Scottish Mission, and the Catholic Missions, specially the Jesuit order. However, in the 20th century, there has been a progressive slackness in the vision which the early mission had. As a result, the missionary concept of education today is understood differently from the traditional view, as we see from the following concept.[48] The traditional view about education is that it occurs during childhood. However, according to many educationists, this point of view is now outdated. What is said to be particularly important in contemporary life, is that people be made capable of adjusting effectively to the rapid and pervasive changes that are already occurring and likely to continue for a considerable time. What is therefore needed is provision of systematic purposeful learning in a variety of settings for all ages.[49] So, while we critically analyze the educational approach of the missions in today's India, the main aim in bringing them to Christ is that we have to take into account such areas as illiteracy, elementary education, adult education (formal and informal), technical and vocational education and study their impact in the communication of the Gospel to the children, youth and adults. The educational approach to the Rajbongshis and the Mising tribe is the most easy and effective way. Christians schools today need to have great concern for the Rajbongshis and Rising tribes in Assam, India. It is not for producing mere intellectual giants or an elitist group of self centered persons who exploit the society for personal gains.[50] It has to produce a group of persons who have to learn in order to serve the society because they are committed to following the service oriented life of Jesus Christ. Education does not mean merely acquiring bookish knowledge. It should enable a person to understand a socialization process. Again, a Christian educational institution should aim at bringing them into the saving knowledge of Christ. The Misings and Rajbongshis have been neglected by the Assam Government in the field of education, specially in among these two tribes in upper and lower Assam. The state of Nagaland has been Christianized through education by the early missionaries. Therefore, it is essential to understand how to reach out to the Rajbongshis and Mising with the Gospel. It will depend on how much qualitative and quantitative education is being imparted to them.

D. Serving the people: A world famous example of Christian social witness is that of Mother Teresa and her sisters in Kolkata. She has become a symbol of Christian selfless caring, and one can not omit her in the Church in India. She worked among the very poor of Kolkata and her hard work spread in the world. There are countless people in Kolkata who are very poor. Even while ill or dying, they have nowhere to lie but on the streets. Mother Teresa and her sisters saw them as people in whom Christ lives, and who should be cared for with the love like Christ loved. So they collected the dying of the streets and gave them a chance to die with dignity and with someone caring for them. The sisters also care for lepers and orphans whom they touch and feed.[51] This is obvious to the Biblical mandate of serving the people in a wholesome way. Jesus said in Mathew 20:28,

"Son of man did not come to be served but to serve the people". It is same with mission that tries to bring a transformation to the Rajbongshis and the Mising by presenting the Gospel of Jesus Christ.

ENDNOTES

44. Roger, Opcit. p. 85.
45. Opcit
46. Opcit. p. 85.
47. L. Barlotti, " perspective on world Miission", Goodnews printers, Bangalore, 1998, p. 218.
48. Ibid., p. 217.
49. Ibid., p. 218.
50. M. Ezra sangma, " Mision Mandate "," School approach in Christian Mission in today's India", By E. A. George Moses , N.D> pp. 328- 329.
51. Ibid., p. 321.
52. Ibid.
53. Pirout, Opcit. pp. 70-71.

CONCLUSION

It is an opportunity and at the same time a challenge to do a detailed research on the tribals known as Rajbongshi and Mising for the upcoming generation, should any Christians Mission from overseas try to reach them with the Gospel. So far, no Christian Mission has come out for this purpose; hence no other research has been explored or done. If Rajbongshi and Mising are to be reached out, the Gospel must be relevant culturally, socially and their culture is to be aspired and only the unadjustable elements which violate the essential Christian faith should be discarded. But at the same time, be affirmative about which are adjustable with the Christian faith and the mission agency. All the believers in that society should be assertive in their faith and expression.

Nevertheless, as it has been noted in this work amidst the Rajbongshi and Mising societal crisis Mission work will continue to grow if any mission agency concentrates to present the Gospel among them whole heartedly they could be won to Christ. They are very rich in culture, traditions and customs. Through this work, it is seen that the Rajbongshi and Mising could be reached by Gospel if the following methods be applied while presenting the Gospel:

a) Indigenous Evangelism
b) Acculturation

c) Education and Literacy
d) Serving the people, i.e. helping the poor and needy people of all age groups. It is a fact that very few churches and missions are working among these people and extend to those missions and the churches who are willing to work among them.

If one observes carefully the missionary activities in Assam, especially in tribal groups, then one can see that the Missionary activities have not been sufficiently done among the tribal in Assam - North East India. The reason is the lack of knowledge in local culture. Therefore, in this book writer Rev. E. Narzary has focused the idea and methods of understanding the tribal culture in Assam in order to win the lost soul by presenting the Gospel.

This book will be helpful to God's servants those who are willing to carry the Gospel among the tribal people in Assam in India.

BIBLIOGRAPHY

1. Barlotti, L. Perspectives on world Missions. Good news Printers. Bangalore. India. 1998.
2. Bowen, Roger. So I send you: A study guide to Mission. ISPCK. Deluxe universal Traders. New Delhi. 1998.
3. Bowie, Richar W. Light for the Nations. BAC printers. Singapore, 1993.
4. Brahma, Kameswar. A study of Socio- Belief: principal and ceremonies of the Bodos. Punthi Pustak. Calcutta. 1992.
5. Chaudhuri, Kalyan. New History of Assam and India. Orietal Book Company Private Ltd. Guwahati, 1998.
6. Choran, Chaudhuri Ambika. Varieties: A Collection of Ten Articles, Bholanath press, Bongaigaon, 1993.
7. Das, Lakshahira. Elementts of Education. Part I. Saraighat Photoo types Printers, Guwahati. N.D.
8. Endle, Sidney. The Kacharies (Bodo). Low price Publications. Delhi 1990.
9. Hedlund, Roger E. Mission to man in the Bible Evangelical Literature Service, Madras. 1985.

10. Iswary, Siricharan. A study of the concept of the "the Incomparable God In Deutero Isaiah and in the Bodo traditional religion and its implication for inter-Religious Dialogue." An unpublished M. Th. Thesis submitted Senate of Serampore College. 2000.
11. Muanthanga, P. C. the harvest field of Assam Carrey Research and communication Centre, Shillong, 1996.
12. Narzary, Paresh Chandra. And Assessment of the Impact of Christianity on Bodo people of Kokrajhar District. An Unpublished Thesis Submitted to Union Biblical seminary. 1995.
13. Niebhur, H. Richard. Christ and Culture. Herper and brothers Publishers, New York 1951.
14. Piroet, Louise. Christianity worldwide A.D. 1800 onwards. ISPCK, London, 1989.
15. Ro, Bong Rin and Ruth Eshenaur. The Bible and theology in Asian context. Asia Theological Association, Bangalore, 1948.
16. Sargunam, M. Ezra. Mission Mandate. School Approach in Christians Mission in today's India (A critical Analysis) By E. A. George Moses. Mission India 2000 N.P. N.D.
17. Ponraj, S. D. Tribal Challenge and the Church's Response Mission Research and Education Service, Madras. 1996.
18. Vijayanunni, M. Assam State District profile: Census of India 1991. India administrative service Register General & Census Commissioner